Everyday
Self-Care

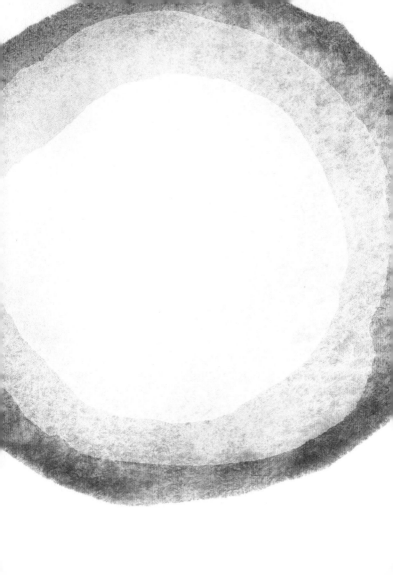

Everyday Self-Care

The little book that helps you to take care of YOU

Compiled by
Dawn Bates

CICO BOOKS
LONDON NEW YORK

Published in 2020 by CICO Books
An imprint of Ryland Peters & Small Ltd
20–21 Jockey's Fields, London
WC1R 4BW
341 E 116th St, New York, NY 10029

www.rylandpeters.com

10 9 8 7

Text © Anna Black, Noelle Renée
Kovary, Nikki Page, Sarah Rudell
Beach, Sarah Sutton, and Sarah
Wilkinson 2020
Design © CICO Books 2020
For image credits, see page 142.

ISBN: 978-1-78249-887-2

Printed in China

Copy-editor: Dawn Bates
Designer: Emily Breen
Commissioning editor:
Kristine Pidkameny
Senior editor: Carmel Edmonds
Art director: Sally Powell
Production manager:
Gordana Simakovic
Publishing manager: Penny Craig
Publisher: Cindy Richards

MIX
Paper from
responsible sources
FSC® C106563
www.fsc.org

contents

introduction

You might be aware that you need to take care better care of yourself, but carry on regardless due to the busy-ness of life. Self-care is something you need to be mindful of and actively plan, rather than something that just happens. This book helps you to do just that: it's packed with quick-and-easy pick-me-ups that will nourish you mentally and physically and help you find a better life balance. Make dipping into this book part of your everyday routine for a daily boost for your mind, body, and soul.

"Be kinder to yourself, and then let your kindness flood the world."

Pema Chodron, Buddhist teacher

your mind

Discover simple ways to feed your mind with positivity, be kinder to yourself and others, and make time for simple stress-busting techniques.

"Talk to yourself like you would to someone you love."

Brené Brown, author and
motivational speaker

being good enough

Self-care starts with being kinder to ourselves. Would you berate your best friend the way you do yourself? We are often our own worst critic—demanding more and expecting higher standards than we would ever dream of asking of someone else. The bad news is that as a perfectionist you will always feel as if you could have done better or worked harder. These constant self-judgments and feeling you are falling short of expectations are exhausting and undermine confidence and self-esteem. Often we want everything to be perfect as a way of keeping control, but life is often beyond our control.

Begin to notice when this need for perfection is arising. What do you discover? How do you behave toward yourself? Do you ease off or press the accelerator to achieve more? How does this pressure affect you? For example, does it affect your sleep patterns, your appetite, your relationship with others?

Once you have begun to notice these thoughts, consider what is driving them—and try to challenge or reframe them. Adopting a "good enough" approach can help to relieve the pressure.

I AM GOOD
ENOUGH.
I LET GO OF
"PERFECT."

finding joy

Choosing to look on the bright side may sound like a platitude—and may seem difficult to achieve—but the new and brighter moments are usually there, and always worth the hunt. The path to happiness lies in our capacity to see the bigger picture, through positivity, hope, and compassion for others. Even in the most dire of circumstances it is still possible to choose your attitude to your situation and retain your sense of identity.

a positive outlook

Our brains have what psychologists call a "negativity bias," which means we pay more attention to negative events than positive ones. This serves an evolutionary purpose, because it means we're attentive to danger, but sadly it also means we miss out on a lot of the small, ordinary joys. Try to pay more attention to the good, and savor the fleeting moments of beauty that life holds. If we can bring an experience into awareness for as little as 60 seconds, we can bank it in our long-term memory. Make an intention to be aware of those fleeting moments of pleasure.

"Ninety percent of long-term happiness levels are predicted not by what happens to us, but by the way your brain processes the world."

Shawn Achor, author of *The Happiness Advantage*

give thanks

Develop the habit of writing down three new things that you are grateful for every single day. Research has found that the simple act will have a positive influence on the way your brains work in just three months.

I have so much to be thankful for.

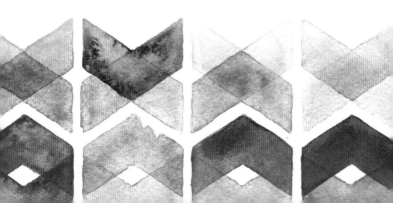

remember to breathe

If you are stressed, panicked, or unhappy, you can usually feel yourself breathing in the top part of your chest. Take a moment to notice your breathing. Then consciously breathe from the lower part of your abdomen. Slow down your breathing and see how quickly you start to calm down. Try to make deep breathing a habit. Be aware of your own breath and take time in your day to adjust it. If you're having an argument or feeling emotional, literally take a few deep breaths—remove yourself from the situation to somewhere a bit quieter and breathe deeply. It really works!

breath awareness

These instructions are simple and taught by
Buddhist teacher and author, Thich Nhat Hanh:

- Become aware of your breath.

- As you breathe in, say to yourself,
"Breathing in, I know that I'm breathing in."

- As you breathe out, say to yourself,
"Breathing out, I know that I'm breathing out."

- You may find yourself simplifying it to "in" and "out."

That's it. Try it.

accepting kindness

Many of us find it easier to offer kindness to others than accept it for ourselves. This practice is a chance for you to be open to the many opportunities when people offer you kindness.

• Notice and acknowledge when someone does you a kindness— it might be something they say or something they do for you or for themselves so you don't have to; it might be as simple as holding a door open or genuinely asking how you are today.

• A person may do something for you out of kindness that doesn't go according to plan—or that isn't as you would have done it yourself. When this happens, notice the judging thoughts and remind yourself of the intention—the motivation behind the action. That is what is important.

• The invitation is simply to notice and acknowledge these moments— allow yourself to accept them with the warmth and care with which they are offered. Sometimes you may want to notice, too, how it feels physically in the body and emotionally.

• Notice your thinking—particularly any thoughts that undermine the kindness, such as questioning motives or thinking that you don't deserve it. Just acknowledge and receive whatever is being offered with kindly awareness and without judgment.

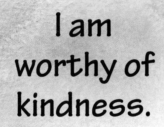

I am
worthy of
kindness.

make time
to meditate

Meditation is a way of giving yourself quiet time. Most people think that it means being able to miraculously transport themselves to a blissful place in the ether. This may be true for some but not many. It is amazing how we all profess to be unable to take 10 or 15 minutes out of our day just to be peaceful, and yet we are unlikely to say we don't have time to browse the internet or watch TV. When you first start meditation, you may find you can barely sit still for 10 minutes. Once you practice meditation regularly, it might be that 20 or even 30 minutes pass by easily. Meditating can leave you relaxed and calm, and you may even find that solutions to problems arise after a session. Meditation or quiet time is food for the soul, and if you feed your soul, the more at ease you are likely to be.

simple meditation

- Find somewhere quiet and sit on a chair with a straight back, or one that has lots of cushions to support your back. If you have a meditation tape, play it quietly in the background.

- Sit with your back straight, but making sure you are comfortable. Gently place your right ankle over your left and relax your hands in your lap, your right hand gently resting in your left palm, or place your thumbs and forefingers together.

- Count up to 60 and just imagine light pouring into your body.

- Count all your blessings in life and ask your God or the universe for guidance in whichever part of your life you feel needs assistance.

- Don't try to blank your mind, but rather accept that a cacophony of thoughts is swirling around your head. Be aware of them, almost like an outsider watching them.

- Concentrate on the light flooding through your body and let peace wash over you.

- When you are ready, count down from 60, then gently resume your day or evening.

noticing guilt

We can be incredibly hard on ourselves when we focus on our shortcomings and mistakes. When you experience guilt, take a moment to notice the feeling and what is triggering it. Is there something to learn from it? Is it a signal that in some way you're not honoring your intentions or values? If so, thank your guilt for providing you with this helpful information, and see what changes you may need to make. See if you can forgive yourself, remind yourself that no one is perfect, and honor yourself for doing the best you can.

I AM DOING THE

BEST I CAN.

laughter

Do you remember what it feels like to shake with uncontrollable laughter; to feel consumed by the joy of a single moment, shared with someone you care about or can have fun with? Laughter wipes away tension in a single breath and turns a frowning face into one that is alive and beautiful. It doesn't take much to trigger a giggle: just thinking about something funny that has happened in the past can provoke laughter and increase happiness. Phone a friend, tell a silly joke, or read a favorite cartoon strip; look for the absurd in every situation.

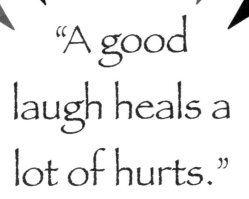

"A good laugh heals a lot of hurts."

Madeleine L'Engle,
author and poet

affirmation exercise

When your headspace feels crowded with unnecessary thoughts and your energy is low, it's time for a pick-me-up. This is a quick exercise to relieve stress, discard unwanted negative energy, and bring focus to the present moment. You can practice this anywhere, at any time. It's not necessary to sit in a meditative state but this will help in the process of shifting your thoughts and energy.

• Find a space that is safe and sacred to you. Make it as comfortable as possible.

• Sit down and breathe deeply, inhaling and exhaling through your nose for the count of five. Allow the air to fill your stomach and expand your ribcage and imagine it traveling all the way up to the top of your crown. With each inhale, visualize your breath creating a golden bubble around your body.

• Repeat the affirmation opposite or adapt it as you wish.

"My intention is to be at peace with myself;
eliminate toxic feelings, elements, and energies
from my life; unlearn negative and harmful
practices and thought patterns; stop checking
for people who don't check for me; create space
for myself that is nurturing for my personal
growth so that I may generate loving energy
for myself and for others; nourish my spirit; and
balance my energies. I have big dreams and
I deserve to live a life I love and let that love
radiate, today and every day I grace the
Earth with my presence."

appreciating
yourself

Everything you need to be happy today or in the future lies within you right now. Wishing you were someone else with other talents and skills, or regretting that you did or didn't make a certain decision, will take you further away from happiness. Looking yourself in the eye and appreciating who you are with all your beauty, skills, and potential will take you to wherever you have the determination to be.

letting go of anger

Anger, rage, and resentment can be all-consuming. They are strong emotions that can take over the body, both physically and mentally. It is natural to feel irritated and angry from time to time, but the irony is that if we hold on to anger, or the feelings get out of control, it will wreak more damage upon us than the person or situation we are angry with. With forgiveness comes a sense of peace and the sense that you can continue with your life. It means committing to a process of change.

forgiveness meditation

If you are struggling with your feelings of being hurt by someone, see if you can practice a silent forgiveness meditation. Bring to mind the person you want or need to forgive and work through the exercise on the facing page. Forgiveness can be a difficult practice, and it may help to repeat this exercise a few times to release yourself from resentment and anger.

- Ask yourself: "Why am I hanging on to my anger? What value is it to me?"

- Now ask: "What would happen if I exchanged my anger for forgiveness? How would I feel within myself?"

- Consider how the situation to date has affected you and whether you have become a victim of your anger because it has become a part of who you are. Focus on thinking about the person who has caused you hurt, and if possible consider their side of the story.

- See whether you can find it within yourself to forgive the person, even if you can't forgive their words or their actions.

You may need to repeat this process more than once, but in shifting your attention to letting go of anger you will gradually become free of the situation that is stealing a part of your life and happiness.

knowing
your
triggers

There are lots of things that can upset us during the day, and it's helpful to know exactly what those things are, because we're often wrong about them. For the next week, keep a "Trigger Tracker" where you write down the specific incidents or behaviors that cause you to "lose it." You might start to notice a pattern: it's always at a particular time of day, or it's because of a particular request, or something else. You may realize that the actual trigger is not what you thought it was (for example, sometimes you might be mad with the kids, but realize it's your husband or co-worker who has really triggered you). Take some time to investigate your triggers and see what you notice.

time of day	trigger/ event	reaction	what I noticed

seven... eleven breathing

Although this short practice is one that is taught to children, we can all benefit from it. Unlike the usual mindfulness of breathing instructions, this practice asks you to breathe in a particular way:

In for the count of seven, and out for the count of eleven.

Try it now and see what you notice. It may take some getting used to, particularly if your breathing is usually quite shallow.

Don't struggle with it, but build it up over a period of time. Practice "Seven... Eleven" as often as you can this week. Sitting on the bus or in the car at a red light, waiting for your computer to boot up or for the kettle to boil. Try to lengthen the out-breath. What do you notice?

this too
shall pass

Remember that no emotion, phase, or pain lasts forever.
Sometimes the ever-changing and shifting nature of the world
is a challenge, and sometimes we can take comfort in the
impermanent nature of our experience.

the mindful minute

People often feel uncomfortable with the open-ended nature of meditation. With this exercise you can create a simple and time-limited meditation tailored to you that can be done anywhere. Simply work out the number of breaths you normally take in a minute and use this as a guide to take a mindful minute at any time you need to during the day.

• Count every breath you take—breathing in and breathing out counts as one breath. Don't worry about the number as we all breathe at different rates. This is to determine the number of breaths you take in a minute, not someone else (and it can vary hugely—in one group of 14 people, for example, it ranged from 7 to 15 breaths). If you like, you can always repeat it a couple of times to get an average.

• Once you have your figure simply remember it and the next time you want to practice, settle your attention on your breath and count each in- and out-breath as one up to the number you determined. That is your mindful minute.

• If you can do this every so often throughout the day, you will be creating minutes of present-moment awareness with all the positive benefits this brings.

I can make
any moment
a mindful
moment.

getting out
of your head

When we are working, most of us spend the majority of time in our head—analyzing, problem-solving, fixing, planning. There is nothing wrong with that when it is suits the task in hand, but too often this becomes our default way of being. When we get stuck in our head, we are unaware of what's going on in the body and so can miss important early warning signals about our well-being. Being grounded in the body also helps prevent us getting swept away by thoughts. Turning our attention to the body is the quickest way to shift our attention out of the head—away from those repetitive thoughts—and into the body, thereby bringing us into the present moment.

simple body scan

This practice is a way of turning your attention to the body. It can be as simple or as complex as you wish. For example, you could just scan your feet or hands if you only have a few minutes. Do this as often as you can to bring yourself into the present moment. You will need to be in a seated position.

- In your mind's eye, draw an outline around your feet where they are in contact with the floor. First one foot and then the other, tracing around the edge of your shoe or foot.

- Move your attention up the body, and wherever the body is in contact with the seat, draw around that area—around the thighs and buttocks, perhaps the middle of the back, possibly the back of the head if it is resting on something. Notice the arms—and if they are in contact with anything (even your body) just mentally outline them.

- Then drop your attention to the feet. Imagine bandaging the feet with a strip of cloth or string. In your mind's eye, wrap your attention around the feet, ankles, lower leg, gradually moving up one leg and then starting again on the opposite side.

- You can continue as far as you want to—perhaps wrapping the torso and the arms. You can wrap the hands as a whole or wrap individual fingers and thumbs.

I am not my thoughts.

a lovingkindness meditation for you

Take a deep breath and place your hand on your heart. Imagine sending yourself as much love and acceptance as you can, and silently repeat the phrases opposite to yourself.

May I be happy.
May I be healthy.
May I be safe.
May I be peaceful.
May I be present.
May I be accepting.
May I be kind to myself.
May I be patient.
May I be curious.
May I be engaged.
May I be hopeful.
May I be loved.
May I be loving.
May I be joyful.
May I be full of life.

what do I need right now?

Sometimes we feel helpless when things are difficult. After honestly acknowledging the reality of a situation and how we feel about it, we may realize that we can't fix it or make it better. As this point we can ask "What would be the most helpful for me to do now?" or "How can I best take care of myself?" This could be something that you find nourishing and pleasurable, something that will give you a sense of satisfaction—or just something that will bring calmness, such as the mindful minute (see page 40).

"Almost everything will work again if you unplug it for a few minutes, including you."

Anne Lamott, novelist

noticing your strengths

On a day when you are feeling emotionally strong, take a moment to look back on some difficult times. Write them down in a journal if you can. Look at what you faced and what you overcame. Remember how you felt at the time and how you felt afterward. Try to bring these times to mind when you are faced with new challenges.

I CAN HANDLE THIS.

count the ways to be kind

We often don't take the time to notice the many ways we can practice self-kindness. Begin to notice what nourishes you—what makes you feel better. Keep adding to the list and begin to intentionally incorporate the suggestions into your everyday life. Pay attention to the simple things that give small pleasures. These are often easier to do than 5-star activities that may take planning and money.

"To love oneself is the beginning of a lifelong romance."

Oscar Wilde, poet and playwright

examples of self-kindness

- allow myself to say no
- slow down
- acknowledge what I do well
- have a computer-free day
- sit in the sun with a book
- listen to my heart
- buy some fresh flowers
- appreciate my achievements
- encourage myself

see through the eyes of a friend

Many of us struggle to see ourselves clearly and we can be self-critical, thinking that we should be better than we are. Try this: imagine you are one of your really good friends or perhaps a grandparent—someone who loves and cares about you and enjoys your company. Picture this person—hold them in your mind's eye and remember how you feel when you are in their company. How would they describe you? What does this person say to you when you are feeling down or struggling?

Write down in a journal whatever arises—there's no need to edit and don't stop until you reach the end of the page. Begin each sentence: "You are..." When you are done, take a moment to read back through the words. How do they make you feel? What do you notice?

"You yourself, as much as anybody in the entire universe, deserve your love and affection."

Buddha

a hug a day

Experts say we need human contact 10 to 12 times a day. It may be the touch of a hand, a tap on the shoulder, a stroke of the arm, or a hug. Hugs are especially stress-relieving. When we're feeling low, getting a gentle squeeze provides comfort like nothing else—there are even therapeutic practices centered on hugging—but, despite this, many of us tend to turn to other coping mechanisms, such as eating comfort food or crashing out in front of the TV.

So the next time you are feeling stressed, sad, anxious, or just generally downhearted, don't turn for comfort to something that is bad for you—instead, reach out for a hug. When it comes to our health, the best thing we can do is open our arms, and acknowledging that you are in need of a bit of kindness and care is an important step.

"If your compassion does not include yourself, it is incomplete."

Jack Kornfield, Buddhist practitioner

hugging yourself

If hugging someone isn't an option, hug yourself with this simple meditation. The gentle pressure on the heart space and the belly stimulates the release of oxytocin along with its benefits.

• Begin by settling your attention on the breath. Allow yourself to experience the sensations of breathing and how the body responds. Use this practice as a way of connecting with the body and with how you are feeling.

• Place the left hand on the belly, just below the belly button, and exert gentle pressure.

• Place the right hand over the heart space on the left side of the chest.

• Keeping the hands in place, focus on the breath. Keep a narrow beam of awareness on the breath, chest, and belly. Really feel the rise and fall and the expansion and contraction.

• Continue for as long as you wish.

color mood
boost

If you are feeling a bit fed up, resist the temptation to camouflage your mood by wearing black. Instead, choose to raise the vibration of your day by wearing something bright and colorful. The chances are, not only will you feel more cheerful, those around you will notice and appreciate the splash of brightness, too.

music mood
boost

What are your top ten happiness tracks? Create your own playlist to deliver instant happiness at times when you need a quick mood boost.

five good things

Before you go to bed, list five good things that happened today. You can do this in a journal, or simply tick them off on your fingers. Even the smallest win ("I didn't have to run to catch the train today") counts!

I DID MY

BEST TODAY.

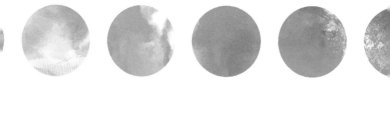

your body

Discover simple ways to take care
of your physical health and eat well,
including delicious and nutritious
health-giving recipes.

"When the well's dry, we know the worth of water."

Benjamin Franklin, Founding Father of the United States

get physical

Like many people, you may not enjoy exercise and therefore find it difficult to align it with self-care. When it becomes a chore rather than something we enjoy, it can be difficult to stay motivated and easy to find excuses to miss your gym class or lie in bed an extra hour instead of going for a morning run. At those times it can be good to remember why exercise is an important part of self-care.

I WILL STRIVE FOR PROGRESS, NOT PERFECTION.

why exercise is so good for you

There are many health benefits from regular exercise:

- Your heart is a pump, which needs to be exercised to work at its best.

- When the blood is circulating properly around the body, it supports all the essential organs of the body.

- Good circulation also clears out the waste and toxins in the body and increases the level of oxygen to the body and brain.

- Exercise provides stress relief and triggers the release of "feel good" chemicals, such as dopamine, endorphins, and serotonin.

- It helps you to control your weight, allowing you to eat more of what you love.

- Exercise helps you sleep better and gives you more energy.

To make exercise part of your life, set yourself realistic goals. Telling yourself you're going to exercise daily is setting yourself up for failure. Start small and add more to your exercise regime as you become fitter.

adjusting your posture

When did you last check your posture? Are you often hunched over? Do you slouch when you sit? Get used to checking in regularly with your posture throughout the day. Our external posture often reflects our internal state of mind. Notice the connection between the mind and body. Familiarity with how your posture reflects your state of mind—both positively and negatively—allows you to make adjustments. Consciously sitting tall can help connect you with the strength of your "inner mountain." You can also do this practice while standing and walking. Notice how you hold your head and how this influences your mood. Experiment and see what you discover.

sitting tall

• Sit in a chair with your feet flat on the floor. Imagine a silken thread running all the way up the spine, along the back of the neck, and out through the crown of the head.

• Give this "thread" a gentle tug so that your spine straightens, the crown of the head lifts toward the ceiling, and your chin becomes slightly tucked in.

• You are now sitting tall, the lower half of the body grounded and connected to the earth beneath your feet and the torso rising up like a mountain peak.

release tension

The body holds tension. When we feel anxious, our breathing
becomes shallow and our shoulders rise. By taking deep breaths and
shaking out the shoulders, you will release tension, improve your
posture, and immediately feel lighter and happier.

I BREATHE AND
I KNOW THAT I AM
BREATHING.

snack attack

When it comes to snacks, it makes sense to remove temptation. If you have only food that's good for you in the house, then that's what you'll eat. It's much harder if you're feeding other people, but everyone will benefit from healthy food. You may find that eating purer food, and more fruit and vegetables, affects the atmosphere of your household. Plenty of scientific evidence exists to show that refined sugar affects mood swings. Some experts suggest that refined sugar should come with a health warning as grave as that associated with cigarettes. So what can you snack on instead?

ideas for healthy snacks

- Hummus with raw carrots or celery. Carrots are a lovely sweet vegetable and delicious raw for a mid-morning or mid-afternoon snack.

- Crackers with hummus and a great dollop of freshly chopped parsley—parsley is very tasty and also provides masses of natural calcium for healthy bones and teeth.

- Nuts—almonds, brazils, and hazelnuts are particularly good, but minimize salty nuts.

- Canned sardines—hugely nutritious and great on a piece of toast with a squeeze of lemon and a handful of chopped parsley, or in a stir-fry.

- Toast with butter and nut butter. Nut butter is a great snack because it gives you some protein.

- Casseroles and soups—have a cook-up and freeze them so you've always got something yummy to eat.

- Fresh fruit—keep it in the fridge so it's always available but doesn't spoil.

the fennel
trick

At one time or another, most of us have eaten too much in one meal and instantly felt bloated. Luckily, there is an easy fix for a stuffed and bloated tummy: fennel. One of the simplest ways to incorporate it into your diet is to chew about 20 fennel seeds after a meal. Fennel helps to digest heavy sauces and carb-centric dishes, which is why you see a bowl of fennel seeds at the exit of many Indian restaurants.

Drinking warm water will also help lessen the bloat.

eat mindfully

When we pay attention to our eating habits, we may notice that we usually eat while doing something else: watching TV, checking social media, or talking to someone. We might multi-task and eat standing up or while we're loading the dishwasher. Too often we eat mindlessly. We pay little attention to the experience of eating and become disengaged with it. The result is we are less likely to pick up on the physical cues that we are full, and so eat too much. We also deprive ourselves of the tastes, sounds, smells, and textures associated with it that add up to savoring the richness of the experience.

When we reach for the cookie jar or help ourselves from the fridge while on autopilot, we are not making an informed choice. When we are on autopilot, unhealthy patterns such as overeating in response to emotional crises are more likely to happen. You can begin to lay down healthier behavior patterns by choosing to make eating a practice.

a mindful eating practice

• Begin with preparing the food. Turn off the radio or television and give your full attention to what you are doing. Chop the onions and feel the smart in the eyes; experience the crunch of the celery, the fresh smell of the lettuce as you break it open. It doesn't matter what the food is, the instruction is simply to be present.

• Notice the "ahhh yummy" or "icky, yuk" response of the body, becoming aware of any thoughts, emotions, and felt sensations that arise.

• When you come to eat, if possible try to be silent. Give your full attention to the experience. Savor the smell, noticing the saliva in the mouth as the anticipation rises in the body. Make the intention to take a mouthful and be with that experience, chew it, and eventually swallow it. Continue in this way, engaging all the senses: sight, sound, touch, taste, and smell.

• When you have finished, reflect on what you noticed.

notice emotional eating

When you find yourself reaching for that extra cookie or piece of chocolate, pause. Simply acknowledge what is happening without judging. Become aware of how you are feeling emotionally, any thoughts that might be present, and any physical sensations in your body. It is important that you don't judge yourself, but simply bring your attention to the breath, breathing in and out a few times before expanding your attention to include the whole body once more. Then, acknowledging all you have noticed, make a decision about what you want to do next. It is your choice and you are the only person who has the power to do something different in that moment. Whatever decision you make, be with it. So if you do choose the treat, be fully present with the experience of eating it, savor it, and let go of any judgment.

I have
a choice.

good sleep hygiene

Make sleep a priority and make changes that will support rather than undermine your ability to sleep.

cool down

Body temperature plays an important role in sleep. We fall asleep as our body temperature drops, and a lower body temperature also helps us to stay asleep before it begins to rise in the early hours as we waken. You can encourage a drop in body temperature deliberately by taking a hot bath or shower about an hour before bedtime and then making sure your environment is cool (about 63°F/17°C). As the body cools, you will begin to feel sleepy. Ideally, exercise no less than 4 hours before going to bed, to avoid elevating your core temperature.

environment

Sleep in a cool, dark room that is free of technology and has a comfortable bed. Turn any clocks to the wall to avoid watching the minutes in the early hours.

keep to a regular schedule

Stabilize your circadian rhythm by going to bed and getting up at the same time—even at weekends and when on vacation.

listen to your body

If, once in bed, you are awake, be awake. Read, get up, meditate, or do some yoga or other calming activity.

notice what you eat

Certain types of food eaten too near bedtime can affect your sleep, but they can affect everyone differently, so pay attention to what you eat. Avoid stimulants, too: alcohol, caffeine, nicotine, and other stimulants are best avoided in the evening and perhaps even in the afternoon.

reduce screen time

Avoid screen time (including television and cellphones) for an hour before bedtime, if possible.

Protect your wind-down time

Notice what helps you to move from the busy-ness of the day to winding down toward bedtime. Avoid or keep to a minimum activities that keep you buzzing. However, notice if there is a sense of striving when it comes to doing particular activities or behaving in a particular way, with the expectation that they will lead to a good night's sleep. This is unhelpful too.

a little bit of sunshine!

Exposure to sunshine is crucial to self-care. Sunlight triggers the body's production of vitamin D, "the sunshine vitamin," which has amazing health benefits, such as lowering blood pressure, protecting against inflammation, and improving brain function, as well as minimizing depression and improving sleep quality. Unfortunately, it's very hard to get enough vitamin D from your diet so try to get exposure to sunlight for at least 10–15 minutes daily.

"Keep your face always to the sunshine, and shadows will fall behind you."

Walt Whitman, poet

self-massage

If there's no one around or willing to give you a massage, try doing it yourself. Stand on a towel in the bathroom before you begin.

• Pour massage oil into the palms of your hands, the more oil the better! Cover your entire body.

• Using small circular strokes, massage the crown of your head. If you don't want oil in your hair, begin the massage at your ears. Avoid using the oil on your face, except for your ears and neck.

• Using upward strokes and an open hand to create friction, massage the front and back of your neck.

• Using a clockwise circular motion, massage around your breasts/chest, then massage your stomach/abdominal area (take extra care if you are pregnant or recovering from surgery).

• Using long up and down strokes, rub one of your arms to create friction and heat. Once you have created heat, massage the entire arm with a circular motion, starting at the bottom of the wrist and working upward toward the heart on the inside of the arm. Repeat on the other arm.

• Add some extra oil to your hands and, without straining, reach around to your back and spine and gently massage with up and down strokes.

• Vigorously massage up and down your legs up to create friction and heat. Focus on the top of one thigh and work your way down the leg, taking care to work your hands in a circular motion on the insides of your legs. Repeat on the other leg.

• Take some extra time to focus on your feet. Really work the oil into your feet and don't leave a single toe untouched.

• Once you've finished the massage, take a warm shower or bath for as long as feels comfortable. The idea is to open the pores to let the oil sink in deeper. Don't use soap to wash off the oil (it's not necessary).

• Towel dry after you shower or bathe. Take care when stepping out of the bathtub or shower, as the floor may be slippery.

wine o'clock?

If you've been drawn into the "wine o'clock" culture—
the belief that you deserve a drink at the long of a
hard day—just be aware of how this might impact on
your self-care. "Just one glass"–one home-measure
large glass–equates to three standard drinks. And
although the health risks start out small, they will
gradually creep up. Be aware that the high you get will
be followed by a low, as alcohol is a depressant. As
part of your self-care regime, it's worth keeping an eye
on your intake and, at least some of the time, looking
for other ways to reward yourself after a long day.

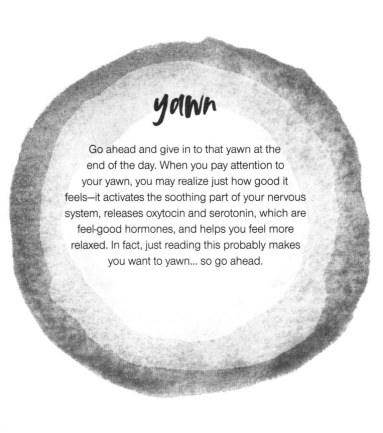

yawn

Go ahead and give in to that yawn at the
end of the day. When you pay attention to
your yawn, you may realize just how good it
feels—it activates the soothing part of your nervous
system, releases oxytocin and serotonin, which are
feel-good hormones, and helps you feel more
relaxed. In fact, just reading this probably makes
you want to yawn... so go ahead.

daily stretches

These simple yoga practices can be done daily to release stress, improve mobility, promote healthy circulation throughout the body, open up energy in the lower spine, massage internal organs, and aid digestion.

spinal flex

This pose is great for anyone who does little to no movement during their day, particularly those who are stuck behind a desk all day or who spend all their time driving around in a car. You don't even have to get up! You may do the Spinal Flex as a five-minute break throughout the day.

• Sit in your chair with a straight spine. Place both feet flat on the floor, about hip-width apart. Place your right hand on your right knee and your left hand on your left knee. Your arms should be activated but not stiff.

• Begin breathing in and out of your nose, filling your belly with each breath and releasing and pushing your navel to your spine. On the inhale, focus on filling your entire diaphragm. On the exhale, try pushing your breath to the back of your throat and down. (The exhale should sound like a hiss). It's okay if you don't get the breath right the first couple of times; with practice, it will come. It is essential to create an internal awareness during yoga, not only to reap the greatest benefits but also to prevent injury to the body.

• With each inhale, arch your spine forward, lifting your heart space upward and pulling your shoulders open and back. Keep your head still and shoulders relaxed.

• With each exhale, focus on pushing the breath out of your body while arching your spine back in the shape of a C. Roll your shoulders forward and tuck your navel toward your spine.

• Do this five times or as many times as you need to feel relaxed and tension free.

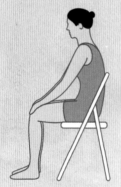

seated spinal twist

Twisting the spine has many benefits. It massages the abdominal muscles and organs, promoting digestion, and keeps the spine healthy. The spine builds up tension between the vertebrae that can cause stagnation and when we twist the spine we release the hidden tension. This wonderful pose helps move energy downward.

• Sit on the floor with your right leg outstretched and your left leg bent at the knee with your left foot on the floor. Lift your butt cheeks and push them out to the sides so you can really feel your sit bones—this helps to lengthen the spine.

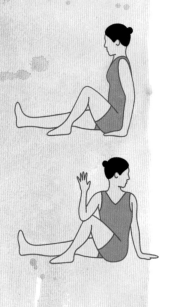

• Inhale, raising your arms up to lengthen your spine and twisting to the left toward the bent thigh, compressing your belly against the thigh. Allow your left hand to rest behind you as if it's a support for keeping your spine straight—you don't want to hunch over. Press your right elbow into the left thigh or knee to increase the stretch.

• If you feel comfortable, turn your neck toward the back of your left shoulder and allow your gaze to follow. Hold for five breaths. Repeat on the other side.

seated forward fold

If you suffer from back pain and intense lower back tightness, one of the easiest methods of relief is a Seated Forward Fold.

• Sit on the floor with your legs stretched out in front of you. Make sure you can feel your sit bones under you and that you are balanced and sitting up tall.

• Inhale, raising your arms up toward the sky and extending them as long as you can.

• On the exhale, lift from your chest and fold forward from your hips toward your toes. Keep your chest lifted to protect your spine; don't collapse. If you can't reach your toes, that's okay, touch wherever you can: ankles, knees, thighs. If this is uncomfortable and your hamstrings are too tight, you can practice this pose using a blanket or yoga block under your tailbone.

• Hold the pose for five breaths and repeat as needed.

warm water with fresh lemon juice

Drink this first thing in the morning to cleanse your bowels, promote digestion, and remove toxins.

½ lemon

1½ cups (350 ml) water

serves 1

Squeeze the juice out of the lemon into a large mug, then add the rest of the lemon to the mug. Heat the water in a small saucepan on the stove until you see little bubbles forming at the bottom of the pan—do not let the water boil. Pour the warm water into the mug with the lemon juice. Alternatively, if you don't have access to a stovetop, feel free to use a microwave. Heat the water in a microwave-safe cup (ceramic is preferred) in 30-second increments. Heating the water in a microwave for 40–50 seconds will usually warm the water to an enjoyable temperature.

gut flush

This recipe stimulates digestion and flushes toxins. For convenience, you can make this mixture at the beginning of the week and store it in a jar in the refrigerator. Take a shot prior to each meal or add it to a glass of warm water.

2 cups (475 ml) water

2-inch (5-cm) piece of fresh ginger, peeled and grated

juice of 2 lemons

2 teaspoons Himalayan pink salt

serves 2

Put the water in a saucepan and bring to a boil. Add the remaining ingredients. Once the water returns to a boil, remove from the heat, cover, and let stand for 2 hours. Using a strainer or cheesecloth (muslin), strain the liquid into a jar and store for up to 1 week in the refrigerator.

oat bran breakfast bowl

This simple dish contains the perfect balance of nutrients for the first meal of the day.

1 teaspoon ghee or coconut oil

1 teaspoon ground cinnamon

1 teaspoon ground cardamom

1 teaspoon ground ginger

2–3 cups (475–700 ml) water

⅔ cup (60 g) gluten-free oat bran

⅓ cup (75 ml) almond milk

½ teaspoon maple syrup

2 Medjool dates, chopped

serves 1

Heat the ghee or oil and spices in a saucepan over a medium heat. Add the water and oat bran and cook for 5 minutes (or according to instructions on the oat bran packet), stirring continuously, until the oats soften and thicken to a porridge consistency. Pour into a bowl and top with the milk, maple syrup, and dates.

raspberry breakfast pudding

Prepare this dish the night before and you will have a delicious breakfast ready to eat in the morning, making for a calmer start to the day.

¾ cup (175 ml) full-fat coconut milk

½ teaspoon rose water

½ cup (120 ml) coconut water

¼ teaspoon sea salt

1 teaspoon pure vanilla extract or powder

¼ cup (20 g) unsweetened shredded coconut

¼ cup (40 g) chia seeds

½ cup (75 g) fresh raspberries

serves 2

In an 8-oz (250-ml) mason jar, add all the ingredients except the raspberries and mix well. Close the jar and place in the refrigerator overnight or for 12 hours. To serve, scoop the pudding into bowls and top with the raspberries. Any leftovers will keep for up to 3 days in an airtight container in the refrigerator.

wake-me-up oatmeal

Self-care begins at the very start of the day, so try to make having breakfast a priority, rather than rushing it or skipping it altogether. This oatmeal made with stimulating ginger and maca and chia, which are nutrient-packed superfoods, will really kick-start your day, and the slow-release carbohydrates from the oats will keep you satisfied throughout the morning.

1 cup (90 g) gluten-free oats (sprouted, if possible)

2½ cups (600 ml) unsweetened plant-based milk

2 tablespoons chia seeds

2 tablespoons ground ginger

2 teaspoons maca powder

2 tablespoons unsweetened shredded coconut

2 tablespoons hemp seeds

2 tablespoons raw cacao nibs

serves 2

Place the oats and the milk into a small saucepan and heat gently for 3–4 minutes, stirring until you have a loose, milky porridge—do not allow it to reach boiling point. Turn off the heat and add the chia seeds, stir well, and leave to cool for 2 minutes. Add the ginger and maca powder and half the coconut, hemp seeds, and cacao nibs. Mix well. It is important not to add the maca when the porridge is at a high temperature as it would lose some of its nutrients.

Spoon into two bowls and sprinkle the remaining coconut, hemp seeds, and cacao nibs on top before serving.

For a raw version of this porridge, soak 1 cup (170 g) raw gluten-free oats overnight in 2 cups (500 ml) water. The following morning, blend the oats and water with the chia, ginger, maca, and coconut. Leave to stand for 5 minutes, then serve with the hemp seeds and cacao nibs on top.

cucumber and dill hummus

In this easy recipe, simply whizz everything together and team with delicious raw veg for a healthy snack anytime.

2 cups (280 g) canned chickpeas, rinsed and drained

2 sprigs of dill

½ cucumber

½ teaspoon sea salt

2 tablespoons lemon juice

1 tablespoon cold-pressed olive oil, plus extra to serve

2 teaspoons tahini

serves 2–3

Combine all the ingredients in a food processor or blender and pulse until smooth, scraping down the sides if needed. Transfer the hummus to a bowl, drizzle with a little extra oil, and serve with cucumber, carrot, and celery sticks. The hummus will keep for up to 1 week in an airtight container or jar in the refrigerator.

good-for-you guacamole

This easy guacamole recipe is special because it contains half the fat of regular guacamole, making it easier to digest and enjoy. Serve it over mixed salad greens or with grainfree chips (crisps) or crackers.

½ cup (70 g) diced avocado

1 cup (175 g) diced and steamed asparagus

juice of ½ lime

½ cup (60 g) chopped red onion

¼ teaspoon sea salt

2 teaspoons ground cumin

½ teaspoon ground black pepper

serves 4

Combine all the ingredients in a food processor or blender and blend until smooth. The guacamole will keep for up to 2 days in an airtight container or jar in the refrigerator.

tropical smoothie

What better way to brighten your day than with a taste of the tropics? This smoothie will keep you satiated with healthy fiber.

1 large banana, peeled and chopped

½ cup (120 ml) half-fat coconut milk

juice of 1 lime

½ teaspoon ground cardamom

½ teaspoon ground turmeric

serves 1

Combine all the ingredients in a food processor or blender and blend until smooth. Pour into a glass and enjoy!

detox smoothie

Start your day with this cleansing smoothie.

2-inch (5-cm) piece of fresh ginger, peeled

juice of 1 lemon

2 Granny Smith apples, halved and cored

2 cups (140 g) kale, chopped

1½ cups (350 ml) water

serves 1

Combine all the ingredients in a food processor or blender and blend on high speed until smooth. Pour into a tall glass and serve immediately.

lemon, rose, and poppy seed muffins

These muffins are a healthy version of a bakery classic, plus they have the added beauty benefit of rose water. Muffins are easy to bake ahead of time, making them a great snack to grab when you are on the go.

½ cup (45 g) coconut flour

½ teaspoon baking soda (bicarbonate of soda)

1 tablespoon poppy seeds

1½ tablespoons grated lemon zest

juice of 1 large lemon

3 tablespoons rose water

⅓ cup (75 ml) melted coconut oil, plus extra for greasing

4 drops liquid stevia

½ cup (120 ml) unsweetened almond milk

3 eggs

makes 12 muffins

Preheat the oven to 325°F/160°C/Gas 3. Make sure all your ingredients are at room temperature before you start making the batter. Grease a 12-cup nonstick muffin pan with coconut oil. In a large bowl, combine the flour, baking soda (bicarbonate of soda), poppy seeds, and lemon zest. In a separate large bowl, combine the lemon juice, rose water, oil, stevia, milk, and eggs. Pour the wet ingredients into the dry ingredients and mix well. Spoon the batter into the cups of the prepared muffin pan. Bake in the oven for 20–25 minutes, until golden brown and a skewer inserted into the center comes out clean. Remove from the oven and let cool in the pan. The muffins will keep for up to 1 week in an airtight container in the refrigerator or up to 1 month in the freezer.

lavender and coconut cookies

These cookies contain no added sugar, yet are so good that you'll want to eat two per serving.

1 very ripe banana (the skin should be almost all brown), peeled

2 drops food-grade lavender essential oil (such as Young Living's Lavender Vitality essential oil)

¼ teaspoon pure vanilla extract or powder

⅔ cup (45 g) unsweetened shredded coconut

makes 8 cookies

Preheat the oven to 350°F/180°C/Gas 4. Line a baking sheet with parchment (baking) paper. Put the banana, lavender oil, and vanilla in a bowl and mash them together until smooth. Stir in the coconut until the mixture looks like dry mashed potatoes. Using a tablespoon, scoop out 2 tablespoonfuls of the cookie dough and roll them into a ball. Place the ball on the prepared baking sheet and repeat until you have used up all the cookie dough. Using a fork, press down the cookies until they are about ½ inch (1 cm) thick. Bake in the oven for 11 minutes or until golden brown. Remove from the oven and let cool on a wire rack. The cookies will keep for up to 5 days in an airtight container in the refrigerator.

raw cookie dough bites

There will be no more feeling sick and guilty for eating raw cookie dough! This cookie dough is actually packed with protein and makes a delicious snack or topping for yogurt bowls.

1 x 14-oz (400-g) can of chickpeas, drained and rinsed

2 teaspoons pure vanilla extract

¼ cup plus 1 tablespoon (175 g) flax meal (ground flax seeds)

¼ teaspoon Himalayan pink salt

½ cup (120 ml) maple syrup or other liquid sweetener

⅛ teaspoon baking soda (bicarbonate of soda)

½ cup (75 g) stevia sweetened chocolate chips

makes about 16 dough bites

Combine all the ingredients in a food processor or blender and blend for about 15 seconds or until the mixture is well combined, stopping once to scrape down the sides. Roll the mixture into little balls and place in an airtight container. The dough bites will keep for up to 5 days in an airtight container in the refrigerator or up to 1 month in the freezer.

sexy mexican mousse

This dessert is for when you just need to indulge in something with a smooth kick. It contains pine pollen, which, when taken over a long period, may increase strength and stamina.

¼ teaspoon chipotle chili powder

1 teaspoon pine pollen powder

2 ripe avocados, peeled and stoned

½ cup (50 g) raw cacao powder

½ cup (120 ml) full-fat coconut milk

⅓ cup (75 ml) maple syrup

1 teaspoon ground cinnamon

2 teaspoons pure vanilla extract

serves 2–3

Combine all the ingredients in a food processor or blender and blend until completely smooth. Taste and adjust the seasoning if necessary. Spoon the mixture into 2 or 3 small serving dishes and chill in the refrigerator until set. The mousse will keep for up to 5 days in the refrigerator.

gentle detox tea

This tea works wonders if you have been indulging a little too much. It promotes a gentle full-body detox, facilitates fat-burning, and aids in digestion of proteins.

4–5 cups (950 ml–1.2 liters) water

½ teaspoon cumin seeds

½ teaspoon coriander seeds

½ teaspoon fennel seeds

½ teaspoon manjistha powder

serves 4

Put the water in a saucepan and bring to the boil. Add the remaining ingredients, cover, and let boil for 5 minutes. Using a strainer or cheesecloth (muslin), strain the tea and pour into a thermos. Take small sips of the tea throughout the day or drink 1 cup (250 ml) of the tea before or after meals.

quiet mind tea

This tea's combination of four herbs works on the nervous system to calm feelings of being on edge and will instantly send you into a blissful state of relaxation.

1 tablespoon dried brahmi leaf

1 tablespoon dried lavender flowers

1 tablespoon dried chamomile flowers

½ tablespoon dried valerian root

2 cups (475 ml) boiled water

raw honey, to taste

serves 2

Put the herbs and boiled water in a bowl and let the mixture steep for 5 minutes. (If you oversteep the herbs, this tea will become very bitter and won't be as pleasant to drink.) Using a strainer or cheesecloth (muslin), strain the tea and pour into a thermos. Once the tea has cooled to a warm temperature, add the raw honey and enjoy!

a good night's sleep milk

This milk is the perfect tonic if you ever suffer from insomnia. Pair it with a warm bath or sleep ritual to enhance the dreamy vibes. The ghee is grounding and nourishing, which is perfect right before sleep.

1 teaspoon ghee

½ tablespoon ashwagandha powder

½ tablespoon mucuna pruriens powder

½ teaspoon astragalus powder

1½ cups (350 ml) warm almond milk (or other nut milk)

1 teaspoon raw honey

serves 1

Heat the ghee in a saucepan over a low heat for 1 minute, then add the herbs and simmer for 30 seconds. Add the milk and stir. (If you have a hand-held milk frother or whisk, you may use it to froth the milk.) Remove from the heat. Once the liquid has cooled to a warm temperature, add the honey.

your life balance

Discover simple ways to get the balance right, add some joy to your life, and do more of what you love.

"When you recover or discover something that nourishes your soul and

brings joy,
care enough
about yourself
to make room
for it in
your life."

Jean Shinoda Bolen, Jungian analyst and author

just being

Are you someone who is always busy and on the go? How often do you give yourself the gift of time—the time just to pause without any agenda and simply create some space for yourself? Taking a moment and intentionally being still, allowing ourselves to be with whatever is present, is a simple practice we can do at any point, anywhere, for any length of time. How do we do this? The easiest way is to let go of trying to do anything in particular and allow things to be exactly as they are. It's the opposite of "doing," which most of us are experts at!

I will focus on
what I can control
and let everything
else go.

learn to say no

Busy people tend to say yes to things just because they can. Unassertive people tend to say yes to things because they can't quite manage to say no. A simple sentence, such as, "I won't be able to do that for you because I am already very busy/fully committed/doing something else," will get you out of trouble.

"Love yourself enough to set boundaries. Your time and energy are precious. You get to choose how you use it. You teach people how to treat you by deciding what you will and won't accept."

Anna Taylor, author

nurturing friendships

As we get older, it can be all too easy to lose touch with our friends, but good friendships are a vital part of our overall well-being and happiness. Rather than going it alone, it's important to be able to share our problems and seek support.

Make a point of thinking about your friendships. Which ones do you value and why? Who would you turn to in a crisis—or to have a great time? Think of your circle of friends as King Arthur's knights of the round table: who would be sitting around the table with you, and why? When you bring each friend to mind, ask yourself why you value that person, and whether you have done enough to show how much he or she means to you. Do your friends know that you value them so highly? Perhaps it's time you let them know. How can you make more time in your life for friends and have more meaningful communication? For example, perhaps you can agree to talk on the phone regularly rather than exchanging brief text messages.

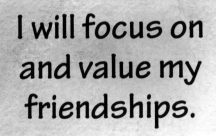

I will focus on
and value my
friendships.

be creative

Make time today for something that's creative or artistic. Color or paint with your child, turn on some music and dance, write in a journal, work on a scrapbook, arrange some flowers, do some baking, or something else that gets your creative juices flowing! When we focus our attention on a creative task, we often enter a state of meditative absorption called "flow," which the research tells us is a very pleasurable state, and one that frees the mind to think in new ways.

smile a
little smile

When we are anxious or stressed, we tense up—often in the shoulders, the jaw, or around the forehead. There is a sense of tightening.

We can practice cultivating the opposite by softening inside. Imagine you are smiling inside. The lips soften, the throat opens, and there is a sense of release. You can take this further by intentionally making eye contact and smiling at people you meet. Can you smile inside today?

you and your phone

The benefits of smartphones are huge—we can stay connected with others regardless of where we are, save time by shopping online, have the latest news at our fingertips—but we can also become enslaved by them. Noticing how you relate to your phone can highlight unhelpful patterns that can impact negatively on your well-being.

time to detox?

The easiest way to tell if your relationship with your phone needs recalibrating is to notice how you feel if you lose it or leave it at home when you go out. If there's a sense of panic or fear of missing out, then things have got a bit out of hand.

phone health check

- How often do you check your phone?

- Where are you and what you are doing when you check it?

- What mood are you usually in when you become aware of the impulse (bored, stressed, anxious, calm, happy...)?

- What you are doing—checking emails (personal or work), social media, shopping, watching videos?

- How long do you usually spend on your phone at any time?

- How do you feel after being on your phone? Does it nourish you or drain your energy?

Remember you are simply gathering feedback—you would usually do these things unconsciously and so if you can begin to notice the context and the impulse, you can start making more conscious choices. Often it is only minor calibrations that are needed to shift an unhealthy relationship into one that is more balanced.

nature lesson

Apart from the physical exercise of gardening, being outside instantly expands our perspective and encourages us to look outward rather than stay stuck in internal overthinking.

There is much to learn from nature. However freezing and gray winter is, the day will come when we notice a bud breaking, feel the warmth of the wind rather than its chill, and realize that the weather has shifted. The natural world reminds us that everything passes at some point.

Being outdoors is a sensory rollercoaster that can place us right in the present moment: the damp potting compost running through our fingers, the sharp tang of a freshly torn basil leaf, the sweetness of a picked strawberry, the sighing of the wind through the trees...

Gardening is an opportunity to nurture—to plant a seed, care for it as it sprouts, support it as it grows tall, and appreciate its beauty or bounty. We can benefit from gardening, whether or not we have a garden. Wherever you live, there is always room for a pot on a window sill. Planting seeds is a great opportunity to grow your mindfulness.

nourishing nature

No matter where you live, spending time outdoors is one of the most precious things you can do. Even in the most built-up areas, something wonderful will be growing somewhere. Plants have a regenerative quality. They give us hope. The fact that something is growing stills the mind and relaxes the body. Try to plan your time so that you venture out of doors every day.

"I go to nature to be soothed and healed, and to have my senses put in order."

John Burroughs, essayist and naturalist

do something different

Memory expert Tony Buzan says that the mind tends to remember things that are different, not things that are the same. So if your routine is unchanged day to day, you will begin to become complacent, because you will no longer notice what you are doing. Making the effort to do things differently occasionally, or swapping responsibilities, or saying thank you with a surprise gesture, will stay in the mind for a long time and have a great impact.

ways to change it up

- Take a different route.

- Choose a different seat.

- Cook something different. Eat something different. Drink something different–a different brand, flavor, topping.

- If you usually eat your lunch indoors, try going outside (or vice versa). If you usually read a book or listen to music on your commute, what happens if you simply sit with the experience without any distraction?

- Make eye contact with people.

- Wear a color or pattern you would normally avoid.

- Shake up your timetable—go to the shops or gym at a different time than usual, or leave the house a few minutes earlier or later.

a room with a view

What do you see when you look out of your windows? Is the outside
area clean and tidy? Are there plants and flowers? You may not be
able to control how your neighborhood looks, but you can make
choices about your home environment and influence how it looks. If
you are really busy, it can feel like just another thing to do and a low
priority one at that, but investing some effort in improving what you see
out of your window will feed your soul.

- If you have a garden or yard, love and cherish it. Expensive plants are not necessary to make it beautiful. Wild cornflowers and poppies are stunning, as are bluebells, cow parsley, and rock plants. It doesn't matter where you live, something will grow naturally.

- If you have no garden or yard, do you have space for a pot or two, or a window box? You can even grow herbs or vegetables. There is little as delicious as something you've grown and nurtured yourself.

- For inspiration, walk in a park and submerge yourself in the beauty of the different seasons. Take a close look at the amazing colors and textures that nature gives us.

candles

A gift to yourself of a scented candle carries a silent message—relax and pamper yourself. You can also turn your home into a relaxing haven using aromatic oils. They are readily available and last for ages in a burner, particularly if you buy the waxy ones that melt. Use votives to heat the oil. You can also create your own scents by mixing aromatherapy oils to suit your mood. Ylang ylang, jasmine, and peony all have a sweet scent that can be uplifting, while rosemary will refresh you and lavender will calm you down.

declutter

How long have you been thinking about tackling those overflowing cupboards and drawers and doing a closet makeover? How often have you turned a blind eye to the chaotic spare room and simply closed the door on it? Thinking about doing a task and avoiding doing a task takes up an incredible amount of energy. So why not just do it today? And think how good you'll feel tomorrow.

"THE FIRST STEP IN CRAFTING THE LIFE YOU WANT IS TO GET RID OF EVERYTHING YOU DON'T."

Joshua Becker, author

the experience of
living simply

If you had only 24 hours left on this earth, would you go shopping or would you want to spend time with those you care about? Money can't buy happiness, although it can, of course, buy fun, thrills, and enjoyment in the short-term. The culture of acquiring possessions, home-making, and dressing well is rooted deep within our psyche and very few people would be willing to give it all up and to choose a non-material way of life in order to achieve happiness. However, material possessions are passive. They cannot love us, or talk to us, or make us laugh—but they do have the potential to leave us comparing what we have with others, and so to feed dissatisfaction, encouraging us to feel nothing will ever be enough.

Take time, right now, to consider all the non-material things that you have to be grateful for. During the course of your life, what or who has made you smile, laugh, feel loved, feel alive, feel curious, feel happy?

- Are you thinking about your love of music, running, climbing, singing, reading, dancing?

- Are you appreciating your friends, your family, your lover, your children?

- Are you remembering places you have visited, the beauty you have seen, the air you have breathed?

- Are you imagining the joy of a kiss, a scent, a taste, or a feeling?

- Are you treasuring a memory of someone no longer here?

The natural pleasures that we enjoy for free make us happy without dissatisfaction or judgment. It is enough that they are there. These are the riches that make us truly happy; and this is the kind of happiness that makes us truly rich.

credits

pp. 16–17, 23, 29, 30–31, 32–33, 38–39, 50–51, 55, 67,
68–69, 73, 80–81, 86, 124–127, 131, 136–137, and 140–143:
backgrounds by IraChe
pp. 19, 42–43, 76–77, 84–85, 138–139, and 144:
backgrounds by Katerina Izotova Art Lab
pp. 26–27 and 56–57: backgrounds by Cienpies Design
pp. 32–33, 44–45, 118–119, and 126–127:
artworks by Julia August
pp. 34 and 58: backgrounds by Veleri
pp. 48–49, 122–123, and 134–135:
backgrounds by Roman Sigaev
pp. 94–111: backgrounds by Elena Nichizhenova
pp. 95 and 101: artworks by Sonya Illustration
pp. 99 above and 105: artworks by Daria Ustiugova
pp. 99 below and 103: artworks by Olga_Serova
p. 102: artwork by Anastasia Lembrik

HOW CAN I BE KIND TO MYSELF TODAY?